Pain Passes
But The
Beauty Remains
Forever

JANELLE VICTRY PAMPHILE

Disclaimer

This book is designed to provide information and motivation to our readers. It is sold with the understanding that the author and publisher are not engaged to render any type of psychological, legal, or any other kind of professional advice. The content is the sole expression and opinion of its author. Neither the publisher nor the individual author(s) shall be liable for any physical, psychological, emotional, financial, or commercial damages, including, but not limited to, special, incidental, consequential or other damages. Our views and rights are the same: You are responsible for your own choices, actions, and results.

The content of the book is solely written by the author. DVG STAR Publishing are not liable for the content of the book.

Published by DVG STAR PUBLISHING

www.dvgstar.com

ISBN: 1-912547-25-2
ISBN-13: 978-1-912547-25-8

CONTENTS

INTRODUCTION 1

CHAPTER 1 MY STORY - AGAINST ALL ODDS 5

CHAPTER 2 FORGIVENESS STARTS WITH ME 11

CHAPTER 3 IT TAKES MORE THAN TEARS TO LOVE AN ADDICT 17

CHAPTER 4 PERSONAL STORY OF A CHILD'S ADDICTION 21

CHAPTER 5 QUESTIONS TO ASK YOURSELF 23

CHAPTER 6 MY FATHERS MESS BECAME MY MESSAGE 31

CHAPTER 7 WE STRUGGLE THROUGH LIFE 39

CHAPTER 8 WHAT SUCCESS MEANS TO ME 43

CHAPTER 9 THE BLACK SHEEP OF THE FAMILY 45

CHAPTER 10 JOY IN TRIALS 51

CHAPTER 11 HOMELESS IN LONDON 55

CHAPTER 12 BUILD YOUR SUPPORT SYSTEM 61

CHAPTER 13 SCOLIOSIS ALMOST KILLED ME 63

CHAPTER 14 MY MOTHER, MY QUEEN 69

CHAPTER 15 HEALING OUR LIVES SO THAT WE CAN LOVE AGAIN! 73

CHAPTER 16 LAUGHTER HEALS YOUR LIFE 77

CHAPTER 17 16 OF MY FAVOURITE MOTIVATIONAL QUOTES 83

CHAPTER 18 QUOTES THAT WILL INSPIRE YOU TO BE 85

CHAPTER 19 MY KNIGHT IN SHINING ARMOUR 97

CHAPTER 20 CREATIVE CHICK FLORIST JANELLE 99

ABOUT THE AUTHOR 122

REFERENCES 123

ACKNOWLEDGMENTS

I would like to express my sincere gratitude and appreciation for the many individuals who helped me throughout my thesis writing process. This includes Erica Daniel, Mother Barbara Clarke, Miguel Clarke, Avanelle, Carlos Clarke, My family husband Linus and children Annalise, Madiba, Ryan, They have provided me with endless support and feedback. I would also like to thank the many kind individuals I met during my time in Trinidad and Tobago, who helped me carry out my project and connect me with useful resources in the region. I would also like to thank the study participants who shared their stories and experiences, this project would not have been possible without you. And finally, to my parents, there are no words to express how grateful I am for you..

INTRODUCTION

My fondest memories is being a captain for my School San Juan girls RC where our team did not win much, but we ended up beating our rivals. The name of the group I led was called Anthodium's. The beautiful pink and white outfits still remain in my head after 35 years of leaving Primary School.

My life mission has become helping others find the mental strength to recognize and take advantage of opportunities, and I have inspired thousands of listeners to have the mental strength to overcome adversity and fear. My purpose is to cultivate drive, focus, and the courage to take action.

In my presentations, I reveal how I overcame my adversities and how I triumphed in my personal life. I take you down a road of lessons that I have learned of hate, anger, resentment, mistrust in adults, violent tendencies, rejection, lack of love, child abuse and the memories that have haunted my life. I believe I have successfully thrived as a leader in life because of my painful past, compassion for others and living a "No Excuse" life.

As a motivational speaker, I inspire youth and adults across the nation to never give up and to not let the past limit their incredible future. I share a message of courage, hope and perseverance to help others find the strength to Never Give

Up. I speak from a passionate soul. I believe that music is one of the purest ways to touch and communicate with the hearts of the audience. I believe it all comes down to a choice and taking responsibility for the direction of your life. I am proof that you don't have to let adversity hold you down in life; you have a fascinating and inspiring destiny awaiting you.

"They told me
I would die ..
I showed them
I can live.."

"Never say that you can't do something, or that something seems impossible, or that something can't be done, no matter how discouraging or harrowing it may be; human beings are limited only by what we allow ourselves to be limited by: our own minds. We are each the masters of our own reality; when we become.".

CHAPTER 1
MY STORY - AGAINST ALL ODDS

I am here to lift up the name of Jesus Christ; the name above all names. What a mighty God we serve! Angels bow before him, heaven and earth adore him, what a mighty God we serve ; I must praise my lord a bit longer. God is indeed a great God.

My name is Janelle Victory Pamphile I was born in a beautiful twin Island of Trinidad & Tobago in the green Valleys of Santa Cruz.

I was born into a dysfunctional family of 3 generations of Alcoholics. My great grandfather, grandfather and my father were all Drunks, and our family's future looked full of doom and despair.

My father was a family man of 7 children and 1 wife. He loved his wife with a passion and his children. His future looked secure as he worked for the biggest care company in Trinidad called Neal and Massy; his dream was short lived as my father's drinking got so bad that he lost his job.

Alcohol is the devil's drink and my father was hooked on it; he did not care about anything not even his family whom he loved so much. I learnt from an early age Alcoholism and Addiction is a selfish affliction, and it does not care about anything or anyone; it destroys the core of our families and communities, leaving broken homes and damaged lives.

My mom Barbara has always been a praying woman that loved her husband and she refuses to feel sorry for herself. Having a alcoholic husband and 7 mouths to feed she knew that the God on the mountain is the God in the valley. She believed that God was her helper and her provider. As a child I would hear my mother crying out to God for help, and she believed with all her heart that all things are possible.

Praise God for the Seventh day Advent Church where we began attending. God answered our prayers and provided us with food, school books, and we had our bills paid. But he provided more than material items; he provided healing for our hearts and souls.

I can remember our Adventist legacy with great joy! I was only 12 years old but I wanted a church that believed in the power on God to cure my Father's Alcoholism.

I ran home with great excitement when I found this church. I told my mum, and her face lit up with anticipation to tell her more; and I told her the Adventist Church was like no other I had been to before.

I believe this Church expresses the true meaning God intended for our lives. The members helped people live healthier lives and they also provided life skills for children and teenagers.

Although my Mum was happy, news reached my Father and he was very angry. He came home drunk that evening. He proclaimed that we were Catholics and that the Seventh day Adventists are cult members.

He called them hypocrites, and my Mum told him that if that is the case, there is room for one more, because the hypocrite was him.

Is that so replied my mother if there are Hypocrites there she insisted my husband there is room for one more. He was so shocked, as he never thought my Mum would stand up for herself. But the spirit of God had planted a seed in our lives. Nothing and no one can hinder the work of the Holy Spirit, and as my Dad's drinking got worse, our faith grew stronger.

Having an Alcoholic father in the Seventh day Church was very difficult; some people never understood and instead were very hurtful and judgmental towards us. I would hear people saying that as a family we had no chance.

But my mum grew her children up to be strong and to use their father's mess as a message to empower people. We believe that no weapon formed against us shall prosper! John 10-10 says, That the thief does not come except to kill, steal and destroy THE BLOOD OF JESUS COVERS IT ALL!!!

Thank God on the 7th July 1997, my mother and 7 of her children gave their lives to the Lord. It was a great day and the entire village came out to support us; but sadly my father did not.

My church family joined together in one accord to pray and fast for my father, as sadly he was very ill and coughing up big chunks of blood night and day. His liver was damaged and I knew he was dying. He looked pale and his eyes were yellow and he had swollen feet. He was only 49 years old.

I believe that the enemy has a hay day with Addicts. He uses denial to the fullest to keep recovery at bay.

For many years my father was tricked into thinking he can

handle his drinking and it was all under control, that he did not have a problem at all, yet he was dying a slow death spiritually and physically.

FOR THE WAGES OF SIN IS DEATH. But the good news is that Jesus never leaves us with hope uncompleted.

"The most beautiful people I've known are those who have known trials, have known struggles, have known loss, and have found their way out of the depths."
~ Elisabeth Kübler-Ross

CHAPTER 2
FORGIVENESS STARTS WITH ME

To know how to forgive, first
I must forgive myself
For everything
I have ever done,
Knowingly or
Unknowingly
That has hurt me and others in any and every way!
Forgiveness starts with me!

The importance of forgiveness

Forgiveness is part of the process of healing and letting go of the past.

When two people are angry with each other, each side feels hurt by the other and would like to receive an apology. Unfortunately, many people believe that they "lose" by admitting they hurt the other person. So neither side apologizes and the mutual resentment can continue indefinitely. It's important to remember that you do not lose by apologizing and admitting that you have been hurting the other person. You win and so does the other person.

So what exactly is forgiveness? We have a lot of

misconceptions about it. For example, that it means being weak, not demanding justice, excusing the reprehensible behavior, or letting oneself be treated badly. It's not any of those things! Forgiveness means to cease to feel resentment against someone or something. It is very empowering to know that you can regain your sense of self. You can wake up each day without reliving the past, even though you won't forget it.

Four myths about forgiveness

1. Forgiving means forgetting. False! Your brain doesn't stop remembering. Instead of dwelling on the past, you are now free to protect yourself and move on.

2. Forgiving means you're a pushover. Absolutely not! Forgiving puts you in a position of strength. You can still hold people accountable, but you take away that person's power to hurt you anymore.

3. Forgiving means you can't get angry. Not true! You don't excuse unkind, inconsiderate, selfish behavior nor minimize your own pain. You can't change the past or predict the future, but you don't have to suffer forever either.

4. Forgiving means reconciliation. Not always! It just gives you emotional space to make decisions that are best for you. It helps you decide, with strength and confidence, what's best for you. You can decide if you want to work things out, or just walk away or do something else.

Why should we forgive?

The Stanford Forgiveness Project has shown that learning to forgive lessens the amount of hurt, anger, stress and depression that people experience. People who forgive also become more hopeful, optimistic and compassionate and have enhanced conflict resolution skills. This research also found that people who forgive report significantly fewer physical symptoms of stress such as backache, muscle tension, dizziness, headaches and upset stomachs. The act of forgiveness also increases energy and overall well-being.

How to forgive

- Acknowledge the pain you feel and recognize who is responsible for causing that pain.
- Express your emotions in healthy ways.
- Release any expectations you have of righting the wrong that was done to you.
- Be mindful to restore your boundaries so that this doesn't happen again. Remind yourself that people cannot give you what they don't have. Remember what to expect of others.
- Find new ways to get your needs met in the future.
- Don't say things like, "I'm sorry you feel that way." This is not an apology, but a criticism.
- Don't make your apology conditional on the other person's apology. "I'll admit I was wrong if you admit you were wrong." Just apologize for what you did wrong. If the other person wants to apologize back, it is their choice, but do not expect it.
- Learning to forgive requires acceptance by acknowledging that what happened really happened, instead of wishing it were different.
- Release the unhealthy attachment you previously

13

maintained concerning how the other person behaves.

- Reframe your life story and find meaning in the broken places. Redefine, recreate and restructure your life.

Forgive others, not because they deserve forgiveness, but because you deserve peace.

Turning Pain into Power

"We are not meant to stay wounded. We are supposed to move through our tragedies and challenges and to help each other move through the many painful episodes of our lives. By remaining stuck in the power of our wounds, we block our own transformation. We overlook the greater gifts inherent in our wounds—the strengths to overcome them and the lessons that we are meant to receive through them. Wounds are the means through which we enter the hearts of other people. They are meant to teach us to become compassionate and wise."
~ Caroline Myss

CHAPTER 3
IT TAKES MORE THAN TEARS TO
LOVE AN ADDICT

It is nearly impossible to love an addict and not to get addicted to trying to fix them. Recovery is needed for both. Loving a drug addict can and will consume your every thought and justifiably so, as you watch them deteriorate both physically and emotionally. Right before your eyes you will watch them vanish and all the while you are also slowly dissolving.

People who are not going through the same thing just don't get it and hopefully they never have to. These will be the folks that will tell you to move on and not to be consumed with your loved one. That is easy for them to say when you are the one living the nightmare. It does no good to get mad. They have no clue what it is like to live everyday wondering if your loved one will make it through the day.

Drug addiction breaks families and brings with it more sorrow than one could ever imagine. Parents live longer than their children, children grow up never knowing their parents, people become homeless and incarcerated. Addiction forces people to live with strangers, who used to be members of the family. Physically, you may remember them but the devil has stolen their soul and they have become someone you used to know.

Drug addiction changes the whole foundation of the family. Each time the phone or doorbell rings, your heart will skip a beat. Is this the news that is so petrifying it takes your breath away? How many social media sites have become shrine memorials for loved ones who have been taken away by a relentless disease that plays by no rules? Drug addiction doesn't discriminate. You will learn to hate the drug but love the addict.

"You were meant to be great. stand in that power."

"No one owes me happiness I owe that to myself.."

CHAPTER 4
PERSONAL STORY OF A CHILD'S ADDICTION

My friend grew up in an alcoholic household and from as early as he can remember, his mother would be drunk and passed out by 6 o'clock. He remembers that growing up, this really scared him and he was embarrassed to have his friends over to the house because he wasn't sure what shape his mother would be in, or what was going to happen at night.

For pretty much every night of his youth, his mother would come into his room and wake him up to ask if she had done anything stupid the night before. She would say she was going to leave the family, or that she was going to kill herself.

For years, my friend said that he would never drink, use drugs, or smoke cigarettes, and if he had been able to stick to that, I wouldn't be writing his story now, but the first time he was offered any of these things, he jumped at the opportunity. He told me that it was an instant love affair and he began using drugs on an almost daily basis soon after trying Marijuana for the first time.

Now I guess the argument could be made that the impossible situation that he grew up in helped to contribute to his initial decision to use drugs, but even in that, there is a fallacy because anyone without the predisposition to alcoholism or addiction would never go near alcohol or drugs after witnessing what it did to his mother.

For instance, my friend's sister stayed away from substances and because of this, she didn't have the problems that my friend had. She was able to avoid the pitfalls of addiction, even though she does drink, and this is because she does not have that predisposition to addiction.

My friend told me that his father once asked him what they could have done differently so that he wouldn't have become an addict, and my friend responded that there was nothing that they could have done. That if his addiction didn't present itself in his youth like it did, it would have come out eventually and that nothing that his parents did or could have done would have changed that.

CHAPTER 5
QUESTIONS TO ASK YOURSELF

Who inspires you?

A: My grandmother. She dances to her own rhythm, she sings to her own tune, and she's lived long enough to know how to love the unlovable and forgive the unforgiveable

1.
....
2.
....
3.
....
4.
....
5.
....

Q: What is the best piece of advice you've ever been given?

1.

....

2

....

3.

....

4.

....

5.

....

Q: What is the best piece of advice you've ever been given?

A: My grandmother told me that quitters never win and winners never quit. That's the way I live—winning is in my bloodline, and quitting was never an option.

1.

....

2.

....

3.

....

4.

....

5.

....

Q: What is the worst piece of advice you've ever given?

A: Let me check from my abundant selection—ha! Tune everything and everyone out and work, work, work.

1.
....

2.
....

3.
....

4.
....

5.
....

Q: What do you know now that you wish you knew then?

A: That success is holistic. It includes my spiritual relationship and physical growth; it's not just my financial and business development.

1.
....

2.
....

3.
....

4.
....

5.

....

Q: What is your favorite quote?

A: "Success is my birthright." I don't know who said it.

1.

....

2.

....

3.

....

4.

....

5.

....

Q: What books are you reading?

A: That's the way I live—winning is in my bloodline, and quitting was never an option.

1.

....

2.

....

3.

....

4.

....

5.

....

Q: What is the worst piece of advice you've ever given?

A: Let me check from my abundant selection—ha! Tune everything and everyone out and work, work, work.

1.

....

2.

....

3.

....

4.

....

5.

....

Q: What do you know now that you wish you knew then?

A: That success is holistic. It includes my spiritual relationship and physical growth; it's not just my financial and business development.

1.

....

2.

....

3.
....

4.
....

5.
....

Q: What is your favorite quote?

A: "Success is my birthright." I don't know who said it.

1.
....

2.
....

3.
....

4.
....

5.
....

Q: What books are you reading?

1.
....

2.
....

3.

. . . .

4.

. . . .

5.

. . . .

"I wonder if I'll look back after you're gone, and wish I'd tried harder to help. But what more help can I give?"

CHAPTER 6
MY FATHERS MESS BECAME MY MESSAGE

How do you fix it?
Alcoholism is a selfish illness

As a family we are at a complete loss at what to do. Your car's broken, bring it to a mechanic. You break your leg, you go to the doctor.

What do you do with an alcoholic?

AA will take you in with open arms once you walk in the door yourself – however, when you're in the throes of a binge that has no end in sight you're not going to walk through that door.

The local doctor whilst helpful in some respects has done as much as he can. He recommended a psychiatrist come to visit Dad, which she did and concluded that Dad was not depressed.

The A&E doctor ticks the patient off his list and sends him on his merry way with a big bottle full of drugs to help in the detox, but no follow up, no suggestion of any other services, if they even exist.

We have organised counselling sessions with an alcohol and grief counsellors, all of which have been cancelled last minute by my Dad.

All of my siblings have sat with him and talked with him about his drinking and how it is affecting his health and our mental health. As a family we have tried group interventions.

When do you walk away?

You can't force someone to get help when it's apparent they don't want help. So what do you do? When do you decide it's time to walk away?

That childhood feeling of dread is back, every day I wait for that phone call.

The logical part of me knows that addiction is a disease, but emotionally it's so bloody hard to understand and accept especially when it's happening to someone you love.
I am a fixer by nature (or maybe by circumstance), if someone has a problem I always try to come up with an answer or a way to fix it. That's why this current situation is so unbelievably frustrating and hopeless.

It's an addiction, you used to tell us, when we still occasionally spoke about these things. It's a disease. I can't help it. I know how seductive that mindset is. And it makes things easier for us, your family, to bear. All the pain you have caused – none of it was personal. But addicts can, and do, seek help. You get round this by claiming they were never truly addicted in the first place. It is more maddening than I can describe.

Drinking is killing you; but you seem to think death is a price worth paying. I don't know how I am going to explain your choices to my children, who will be devastated to lose a grandparent, but I can tell you this: I am not keeping your secrets for you. When they are old enough, I will tell them what alcohol did to you. I am sad, frustrated and angry, but I am not ashamed, and the last thing I want is for them to make the same mistakes as you.

People ask me why I don't just cut all contact. But when you are sober, I see the dad I remember, the funny, fascinating man with a way with words and a knack for telling a story. I suspect you think you are funnier after a beer or six. You are not.

Everyone knows it. Except you.

Allan Micheal Peter's was my father who was an Alcoholic as long as I can remember my father's drinking problem was a great disgrace to the family. He had a good job at Neal and Massy in Movant in Trinidad and was very respected Mechanic. My father could of fixed any car he was deemed the best Mechanic in Trinidad. But he has a serious problem that will take his life. My father was a kind person but regarded his addiction more important than his wife and kids.

Sadly his family would have to pay the price for his addiction because before we could eat his drinking came first. My mother did her best to help her family, she was a very industrious educated woman and my father new that he was not able to assist the family so he looked for a wife who was much educated than him and someone who can carry the fold. Taking responsibility for his actions, he would put the blame on you and see you as the problem, not his drinking.

As a little girl I was very impressed by my father being around the family in spite of his drinking problem because in my community there was always a single mother and the men were never present. It was hard being a daughter of an Alcoholic that really affected my self-esteem and self-worth.
I was bullied at school a lot because my friends who lived in the community knew of my father's drinking but that made me stronger and molded me. I was determined that my father's mess can become my message.

My father was a very respectable man and would show respect to all when he drinks as like a different personality came out of him from being a very quiet man who did not have a lot of friends to drinking to ease his pain.

As I grew older I was very curious about what made my father start to drink in the first place so I just asked him. For a long time he just smiled., but he saw something different in me than all his children and we had developed a great bond, my father trusted me with everything that he had, he would inform me of all his money and I was his accountant and he would try to teach me how to save for the rainy days. I developed skills as a home maker to be able to be in control of the running of the house, which I am very thankful for and used that in my life.

Finally my father was able to open up to me and said his drinking began when his mother left Trinidad for Venezuela to work and he started drinking to ease his pain, he really missed his mother, they shared a great bond. I was for sadden for what I heard it really touched me and allowed me never to judge anyone there is always a story behind the message. I hugged him really hard and said that it's not your fault why she left, he was very touched as well and cried, it was the first time I witnessed my father crying. That moment I saw my father in a different light and I promised him I would help him through till the end.

Although his drinking did not stop as I wanted I was able to talk to him and share how I felt and how his drinking affected me as a child and now my father exclaimed he was sorry for the hurt he has caused all of us including his wife whom he loved so much

Alcoholism is a selfish disease that affects the whole family in every area: mentally, physically, emotionally and holistically Alcoholism breaks the family's institution and divides the beauty of the family until some children grow up blaming themselves for their families addictions and end up destroying their own lives.

My father's drinking lifestyle affected me and my family so much we were very bitter and angry as children and as youngsters. It was the Church, the Seventh Day Adventist Church, that really molded me into the woman I am today. My relationship with Christ that was my only solution to the problem and overcoming my painful childhood. I also saw that my family relationship with each other improved, as matter of fact, my father's life changed and he was transformed.

Dimming your light
doesn't do you or the
world any good.
You were meant to be
great.
Stand in that power.

God grant me
the *Serenity* to
accept the
things I cannot
change. the
Courage
to change the
and things I can
the *Wisdom*
to know
the difference

CHAPTER 7
WE STRUGGLE THROUGH LIFE

We struggle. We strive. We yearn for a better life.
Life is one beautiful struggle or nothing at all.
Do you wish life was without challenges or setbacks?
If that were so, how would you realise your potential without
struggle?

Without growth life is dull and dreary. We strive and struggle
so we may overcome, for it is in overcoming we prevail and
realise our magnificence.

We are endowed with an inner calling to grow and thrive. It is
inbuilt into our genetic coding to grow into a better version
of ourselves. As you reach to become more, you align with
universal intelligence to express your infinite potential.

We play a small role in the greater orchestration of events
which take place in the physical universe. This does not mean
we play an insignificant role in the co-creation process, rather
the decisions we make today have a ripple effect in our lives
and the lives of others.

We are connected at a deeper level through consciousness.
Your beliefs frame your perceptions. Your perception colours

your view of reality, so that what you expect is what you get. It's an ongoing discussion that life is one struggle after another. Yet it need not be that way.

There is more to life than your impression of it. Notice I used the word impression, since the way you perceive the world is clear by your observation of it. Life need not be a chain of endless struggles, paying the bills and being dissatisfied in one's job.

Life Waits Your Next Move

"Quietly endure, silently suffer and patiently wait."—Martin Luther King Jr., Why We Can't Wait
Life offers moments of bliss when we least expect it. The lucky break that comes just at the right time, having devoted much of your life pursuing your passion.

Our struggles pale into insignificance when we're in love and committed to serving others.

Life does not come with a user's manual. I don't know about you, but I wouldn't have it any other way—the joy of overcoming is rewarding and a part of the human condition.

Life offers so much or so little. It is filled with: heartache, pain, emotional trauma and moments of anguish. This is contrast to the moments of falling in love, witnessing the birth of your child and personal victories.

Pain exists to give rise to joy.

The principle of quality contrast and paradox work in harmony with one another. Yin energy is the complement of the Yang energy.

Life is called a journey, for it is the experiences we embark upon that have a lasting effect on our lives.

Life is a series of highs and lows.

The moments of bliss or episodes of agony are a focal point long after the experience has taken place.

We should not assume life will conform to our desires at the drop of a hat, rather allow life to flow through us, unimpeded. We do so by remaining receptive to what shows up, even if we believe otherwise.

The title of this article illustrates the dichotomy of life. Without the struggle, life serves no role towards our personal evolution.

The purpose of life is to create itself anew within each moment. Through chaos life is born, which serves as the impulse for its creative expression. We see this application in nature.

Diamonds are formed under intense pressure, heat and agitation. The turbulent weather patterns recedes to give way to the welcoming spring and autumn months.

We look forward to these seasons rather than take them for granted. Imagine if we had one season for twelve months of the year?

There would be little to appreciate in terms of the contrasting weather changes. Contrast emerges in nature so we may experience different realities.

I invite you to reframe your challenges as analogous to the seasonal changes.

Nothing is permanent.

Painful experiences come and go if we allow them passage through us.

Instead of viewing life as a series of endless dramas, appreciate that your personal battles are leading you toward the realisation of your deepest wisdom.

This wisdom connects you to the same intelligence that is serving you every moment. It might not show up in the way you expect, yet it is always working behind the scenes.

Life can be a series of beautiful struggles or nothing at all.

Call To Action

CHAPTER 8
WHAT SUCCESS MEANS TO ME

Success to me is really living out my days, my months, my years and having no regrets in any area of my life, particularly in my relationships:

I said what I needed to say when I should have said it.
I apologized sooner, quicker, faster.
I said I love you more than enough.
I forgave myself and others effortlessly.
My relationships were bountiful.

Success to me is not shrinking when I had an opportunity to play big even if I was scared, that I took a leap off the ledge, not even knowing if my parachute would open.

Success to me is living out my purpose—that, ultimately, when my time is done, I will have lived every day writing the most amazing story. When I sit down to rest, I will be plum tuckered out because I played full out. I won't take any extra energy with me. I will leave all my wisdom, all my nuggets. I will leave everything here to live and grow.

"That's success to me."

CHAPTER 9
THE BLACK SHEEP OF THE FAMILY

Girl you are so ugly and skinny! Look at you! Nobody in this whole wide world is ever going to like you, not only are you skinny, but you are Black and remember Black isn't beautiful..

Your daddy is the ugliest drunk in the Village, and girl if I was you I would jump in front of the nearest truck.
You don't have a future because your skin isn't light! You are not going to get any job in the bank with that ugly colour you have got. Girls in the bank are all Asians and White, you nigger.

Instead, we could replace our resentment with compassion for ourselves and those who hurt us. Because they are hurt, and unconsciously trying to get others to strengthen their paradigm of pain is the opposite direction of turning towards the path of healing and growth.

SELF ESTEEM, ANXIETY, DEPRESSION, RELATIONSHIPS

"I'm the only normal person in my dysfunctional family, why

should I be the one to get help? They are the ones who need therapy!"

Literally, the most common thing I hear from clients.
The black sheep of the family is the outcast, seen as different, written off. At best, they're playfully teased; at worst, they're rejected. The more they're ridiculed, the less likely they are to open up and share things about themselves. The less they share, the more of an outcast they become.

WHY DOES THIS HAPPEN?

Childhood emotional neglect (intentional or accidental) can cause people to shut down from an early age. Children who get the message that their needs aren't important often become adults who try to "do it all" themselves.

Think about how your caregivers responded if you expressed a need. What was the response if you expressed sadness, fear, enthusiasm, excitement, pride, disappointment, or anger?
How likely are you to express each of those feelings now, as an adult? Have you learned to be vulnerable? Or do you put up walls to protect yourself? Are you bashful about showing pride in yourself?

There's nothing wrong with wanting to be independent - but when you feel like you have no other choice, it can cause feelings of depression or anxiety to build up.

ARE YOU THE BLACK SHEEP OF YOUR FAMILY?

It starts small. You hide seemingly minor things about yourself.

Your family doesn't need to hear about (much less meet) the new person you're dating. Plus, they just happen to be from a different culture. Definitely not bringing them to Sunday dinner.

You haven't mentioned you aren't going to temple/mosque/church anymore. They would make a huge deal about it, even though it's low-key been years.

No, so far the world hasn't ended because I go to brunch instead of praying.

They don't need to know that you're looking for a different job and maybe don't want to stay in the same industry. You're just looking! There's nothing to tell yet anyway.

"They wouldn't understand."

"I hear the way they talk about [person with a mildly specific trait they attribute all that person's problems to], no way I'm coming clean."

"I don't need them, I have my own support network."

"Believe me, if you saw the way they get at family gatherings, you'd understand."

Before you know it, you're hiding most of the real you from the people who, at one time in your life, you thought knew you best.

NOW WHAT?

Ideally, we should be able to renegotiate our relationships with family as we become adults. (This doesn't apply if there are abusive or dangerous factors involved. We're not obligated to negotiate with people who have harmed us.) I know very few people who have been able to do this successfully.

What tends to happen instead, is one of two things:

1.   People stay enmeshed and kind of codependent on their family, even while still being treated as an outcast. In other words, they keep taking crap from them, waiting to be treated better. Or,

2.   They become increasingly withdrawn from their family, to the point where they start to dread holidays and family gatherings. They might rely on them in case of emergency, but that's about it.
Neither of these sounds fun! But don't worry - you can balance things out by trying the following:

RELY ON YOUR CHOSEN FAMILY

Chances are, you connect with these people because they know exactly how you feel, and probably have gone through something similar. Commiserating with someone who gets it can be incredibly validating. Which is important when your family treats you like you're the weirdo. (Also, why are you practically disowned for not becoming a doctor, but your cousin is a golden child because they're a corporate executive Monday through Friday even though they're trash on the weekends?)

SET SOME GROUND RULES

It's not all bad! Can you find some safe topics to talk about together? Decide what events are worth attending (like if your non-trash cousins will be there, it'll be fun). Guess what: You don't have to stay the whole time. You can decide how much time you spend together, what behaviours are deal breakers, and when you're ready to leave.

LET PEOPLE SURPRISE YOU

If you're tired of the same dynamic playing out, chances are your family feels the same way. Try speaking up about your experience and you might be surprised. You can always voice your concerns in an assertive, kind way, and see if your family is receptive. Just like you expect them to act a certain way, they are probably expecting you to be the same person you were 5, 10, or 20 years ago. If you take a chance and show how much you've grown, it creates an opportunity for them to step up to the plate. (OK it might backfire the first few times, but give it some time! If you can learn new skills, so can they.)

BE YOURSELF

The more authentically, proudly, and openly yourself you can be, the less of an effect other people's opinions will have on you. Part of the dynamic is that you are anticipating what your family will say. Let them say what they want, at least you're busy living your best life. Speaking of which...
Listen to your Cheerleaders

We can all name 2 or 3 naysayers who will judge us for a certain choice or behavior. Don't list those names! Instead, list the many more people who will encourage you, support you, and maybe even join you. If a hater gossips in the forest but there's no one there to hear them, do they even matter?? Yes, being the black sheep can be isolating. But it's these experiences that ultimately lead people to be unapologetically themselves.

CHAPTER 10
JOY IN TRIALS

As crazy as it sounds to us, James did indeed mean that believers should consider trials an opportunity to experience joy. He even tells us why.

1.   God's Process – Trials build and grow our faith like weight training does for our muscles. Life's difficulties, Christian persecution, and temptations all put our faith to test. God uses this process to burn away impurities, refining our faith. He builds and shapes our character to look more like Jesus.

2.   God's Purpose – I love the way the NLT translation puts it. When our faith is fully developed, we will be "ready for anything!" God has a specific purpose for each of us Ephesians 2:10). He has a plan, a way He wants to use us for His Kingdom. But He must shape and prepare His tools (you and me) so we will be useful in His hands.

3.   God's Presence – Throughout God's Word, He promises to be with us always and through everything (Isaiah 43:1-2, Matthew 28:19-20). Trials provide an opportunity to experience God's presence in ways we cannot in easy times. If we never have to rely on God, we would never experience

His faithfulness. If we are never weak, we would never experience His strength. Through trials we move from merely intellectual knowledge of God to experiential knowledge. Shared times of trial fosters deep intimacy and dependence. This truth seems crazy to us because we often move through life spiritually short-sighted. We are stuck in this physical world and fail to see the greater reality. God works on an eternal time-table with eternal purposes in mind. He's working for the end game. Let's join Him!

Our own trials will of necessity mean suffering — and there can be little joy in suffering. Joy never has its direct origin in suffering — but it does often come out of suffering, or as a result of enduring suffering. The order in which it works is clearly seen in Hebrews 12:11, "Now no chastening for the present seems to be joyous — but grievous — nevertheless 'afterward' it yields the peaceable fruit of righteousness." This is what you may expect — grievousness in time of trial and chastening — and afterward the reaping of joy.

The Bible speaks of our being "in heaviness through manifold temptations," and also says, "We count them happy who endure." Enduring implies suffering — and suffering, of itself, can never be joyful. We might, in a figure, say that suffering is the soil in which the tree of patient endurance grows. Joy is the ripened fruit of the tree.

There are many different kinds of trials, and they have different effects. Sometimes they are like a great storm that sweeps over the soul, when the dashing rain obscures all view of the distant landscape and its beauties, when the howling of the wind, the flashing of the lightning, and the rolling of the thunder shuts out everything else and holds our entire attention. It is only when the storm is over and the calm has come, that we can look out again upon the broad and peaceful landscape.

There are other trials that remind one of a stone in one's shoe — everywhere one goes, it is present, irritating, annoying, torturing. It hinders and detracts from all the common pleasures of life.

When trials come, there is just one proper way to meet them — that is, with determination to overcome them and to keep our integrity during the time that we are suffering under them. It was the joy set before Jesus, which made him strong to suffer. And so we, if we would be strong for our trials, must look beyond them to the joy that is set before us. It is what is coming out of the trials that is the source of our rejoicing. If you have endured some trial — something that took real courage and fortitude — and you look back upon it and realize that you stood true, that you did not yield nor falter — then is it not a source of great joy to your soul?

When you see the grace that God gave you — does it not strengthen and encourage you?

You desire the peaceful fruit of righteousness in your life — you want joy, peace, and victory; but remember that these are the "afterwards" of patient endurance through the trial or chastening. You must wait for the fruit to ripen! If you try to enjoy it before it is ripe, you may find it works like eating an unripe green apple — you not only will spoil the fruit — but will find some unpleasant consequences.

There are certain kinds of trials that bring forth joy quickly — if they are met in the right spirit. We read that the early Christians "took joyfully the confiscation of their goods," and again that they "rejoiced that they were counted worthy" to suffer for the name of Christ. This was persecution. Often we can "rejoice and leap for joy," not because of the persecution — but because of the fact that great is our reward in Heaven. The joy comes from the contemplation of that reward. We suffer the persecution — and we rejoice in the reward of our patient endurance.

If we walk close to God — then we shall find that in the midst of our trials, even when they are bitter, that there is an undercurrent of sweet joyfulness way down in the depths of our souls. The consciousness that we are the Lord's, that he loves us, and that he is our helper — will be sweet in the midst of all our woes. This may sometimes be obscured by doubts and fears for a time — but if we hide away under his wings and trust securely, the harp of joy will sound in our souls though in the tumult of emotions. We may sometimes have to listen carefully, however, to hear the soft, sweet strains of its melody.

Be patient in your trials!
Endure hardness as a good soldier!
Keep up the shield of faith!
Fight the good fight!

And in due season your soul will sing triumphant songs of victory, and the joy-bells, pealing out their merry music, will summon God's people to rejoice with you in your Lord and Savior!

CHAPTER 11
HOMELESS IN LONDON

Being homeless in London was like living in hell. The street was cold and being a foreigner from the Caribbean made it worst. I was homeless for 2 weeks, from 5 days after my arrival from Trinidad. I was cold hungry and all alone. My mum told me it would be best to come back home, because there is no way I could make it in a white man world...

Maybe my mum was right. People stared at me as if I was from another planet! I was sleeping around junkies; people on crack cocaine, alcoholics and prostitutes. I saw this guy injecting himself with needles in his foot, because he has used up all the veins in his body. That made me really want to go back.

AT NIGHT WAS THE WORST

As a black girl I had to be very vigilant because there was this guy marking my every move to attack me. I was scared, and I was all alone in a big City with no family or friends . In my mind, the Lord said to me to get to my nearest Adventist Church, and maybe someone could help.

I was looking like a homeless girl now, my clothes looked dirty. Everywhere I went people were looking at me and laughing, but there was a strength in me that no one could break!

I almost died when I was 8 years old in Trinidad at 15 I was operated on and was crippled from the waist down and I survived!

If that didn't kill me then I believed nothing would. I gained strength and began to remember the pain I suffered as a child and the people that hurt me and abused me. I believed God was with me through good and bad and that one day things would get better. I started to volunteer at a Charity called Fara. There was something about me that the owner admired, and although I didn't get paid, I was provided with clean clothes and someone gave me some money for a back room in a hotel where I could get some rest.
I am forever grateful for this act of kindness.

Thank you Sir.

COLDEST NIGHT IN LONDON

I thought my life was changing for the better, but something was about to happen! That night in the room next to mine, something happened that would make me or break me forever.

It still rings in my mind like yesterday, the sky looked so dark and scary, I really missed my family and felt so alone and shaken.

But I slept through the night like a baby. I woke up, had a shower and went downstairs to make my breakfast and had a nice cup of tea.

As I was going back to my room, I saw a very tall white man. I quickly said good morning to him and noticed that he had the bluest eyes I had ever seen!

He was carrying a big bag, and he looked at me and smiled. I thought nothing of it, but within a few days the police began calling me, to get information because that same man just murdered a girl in the room next to where I was staying that night.

Silence immediately gripped the room. I couldn't sleep for months. It really affected me, as I felt like I could have been that girl. The man gave himself in and informed the police that he saw a pretty black girl with an accent. My life was never the same, and I am grateful that God protected me from that man.

Loving an addict can be one of the hardest and most trying experiences. Addiction, whether it be to Alcohol or to Drugs, can have long-lasting and negative effect on those closest to the addict. Below are some strategies that can be employed to cope with a loved one's addiction. There is a focus to guide them towards a path of treatment and recovery.

For the person who loves someone addicted to drugs or alcohol, it can be heart-breaking to watch the Cycle of Addiction spiral out of control. Oftentimes, it feels like your relationship is secondary to their addiction. It can leave you feeling powerless before the strength of their addiction and helpless to steer them towards recovery.

The downward spiral of addiction results in the destruction of their life including relationships with those around them, loss of a job, and withdrawal from society. Their actions hurt not only themselves but can also hurt you. While things can seem hopeless at times, there are steps you can take to help both you and the person you love.

ACKNOWLEDGE THE ADDICTION

The first and most important step you can take is to recognize and acknowledge their addiction. Whether addicted to alcohol or drugs, identifying and acknowledging their addiction is the first step towards freeing yourself and your loved one from the cycle of addiction.

While some cases of addiction have clear and present signs, others are less apparent, particularly to those closest to the addict. Look for ways in which the addiction has had a negative impact on their lives and the lives of others including with yourself, others they are close to, their job, and changes to their health and finances. Sometimes looking at the effects of the addiction can help you better understand the severity level of the addiction.

Acknowledging that your loved one may possibly be suffering from an addiction problem can be difficult. The person may not have been an addict when you first met and may have only drank or used drugs occasionally or socially. However, over time your loved one began to rely more on drugs or alcohol to treat the demands or pain they are faced with. An important first step is for you to recognize that there is a concern and consult with a professional to better understand the next step to get the help they need.

SET BOUNDARIES IN YOUR RELATIONSHIP WITH THE ADDICT

Once you have identified and acknowledged their addiction, it is important to set clear and firm boundaries for yourself and for them. You must identify the ways that you may have been enabling their addiction in the past, and create boundaries to prevent these behaviors in the future. For those closest to an addict, it can be difficult to identify the ways they are enabling their loved one's addiction because it can take on many forms.

Developing an understanding of addiction and its effects can help you to see how your actions may be enabling them to continue with their addictive behaviors. Setting proper boundaries in a relationship with an addict is crucial in order to show them exactly how their addiction is affecting the lives of those they love. It is important to commit to your set boundaries and communicate with the person you love why you are needing to change your own behavior.

LOVE YOURSELF

With proper boundaries in place, those who are in love with an addict can move towards loving themselves again. Often the destructive cycle of addiction and substance abuse will take an emotional and physical toll on those closest to the addict. In order to help the person you love, you need to take care of yourself first. This can be particularly difficult for parents, family members, or spouses/partners of addicts.

Loving yourself first is not an act of selfishness or callousness. Rather, loving yourself first allows you to create a healthy space from which you can help the addict in your life. It allows you to be in a better mindset supported by strength and clarity to better help the person you love. Taking a step back from an addicted loved one and helping yourself first is perhaps the most difficult step most people face. However, it is necessary in order to truly help the addict in your life through their process of recovery.

FALLING IN LOVE WITH JESUS
IS THE BEST THING
I EVER DONE!

CHAPTER 12
BUILD YOUR SUPPORT SYSTEM

As part of loving yourself, reach out to those around you for support. Begin to build a network of those you love and who love the addict in your life. Other members of your family, loved ones, friends, and others close to you can help lend strength and knowledge to helping the person you love. Speak with the members of your support system about how the addiction has affected all of you, and take the time to document this information.

Your support system is there for both you and the addict in your life. Even if you are the primary point of contact with the addict in your life, your support system will provide you with a point of stability you can rely on. A strong support network can also help demonstrate to the addict that there are people around them that care about them and want to see their life change for the better.

DETERMINE A TREATMENT PLAN

Loved ones can learn how to be in a relationship with an addict by acknowledging the person's addiction, setting boundaries, empowering yourself, and building your network of support. A strong support network should always include a qualified medical professional who will assist the patient and family through the recovery process.

The professional is instrumental in developing the individual's treatment plan which will greatly increase their chances of a success. A comprehensive treatment plan should include spiritual, physical, and emotional components. In addition, the medical professional will provide guidance to loved ones by providing support and directing them to the resources needed to help the patient along with their journey.

CHAPTER 13
SCOLIOSIS ALMOST KILLED ME

LIFE AFTER SPINAL SURGERY

I sat shivering on a bed covered with stiff sheets, my hair tucked into a surgical hat. My father stood tall and strong with a stoic expression on his face; my mother wept in the arms of the anesthesiologist. Embarrassed, I tried not to make eye contact with people as my bed was pushed down the hall. A set of doors swung op and I heard jazz music playing in the background. A small woman was arranging what looked like garden tools on a table. A mask was put over my face – and then it was over.

As a teenager I was diagnosed with scoliosis. I was 13 years old when my gym teacher sent home a letter suggesting that I may have a curved spine. My mother located a scoliosis specialist. This man was unique – when he entered a room he was followed by a mass of white-coated students who watched his every move. Standing at least six feet tall, he towered over my petite frame. His voice, deep and raspy, brought out my timid side. His professional manner exuded confidence and his knowledge established it.

My doctor confirmed that I did have scoliosis. My spine was labeled a double major curve or S curve. The doctor decided to take a "watch and wait" approach – every six months I came into the clinic to be checked. When I was 16, surgery was recommended. The curve in my spine had progressed to the point where it would become a major deformity if it were left untreated.

Ginny, my doctor's nurse, walked me and my family through the risks and benefits of surgery. She was the "go to" person for questions and a safe place to express fear and frustration. Ginny and my doctor worked well as a team. He spoke the facts and she helped them make sense.

At 16 years old and a junior in high school I was determined that this surgery would not ruin my social life. I explained to my doctor that my surgery must be performed after homecoming, but before prom. I then proceeded to ask that he remove a mole from my back while he was at it. He chuckled, and seemed pleased that I was handling the situation with some confidence.

Vitamin C and iron supplements became part of my daily routine as I prepared my body for blood donation. My mother and I would go to the local blood center once a week where I would donate my own blood for the operation. This process didn't bother me, but my mother would always feel ill after watching the bag fill up with blood.

My mother's strength was demonstrated as she took me to appointments and listened to the details of surgery. She asked embarrassing questions about childbirth, sex and life after spine surgery. My mother advocated and protected me through the entire process. Now a mother myself, I can't imagine the fear and anxiety she must been feeling.

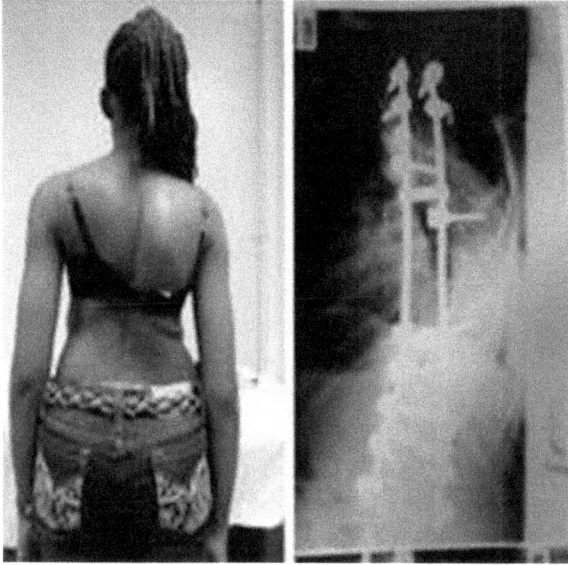

Miracle Hands Dr David Toby

This wonderful man saved my life! He took a big risk operating on a then 19 year old teenager who was very underweight.

I stayed at the Princess Elisabeth Home, and it was the only place in my life as a young person where I felt love and understanding. The nurses cared for me with great tenderness and compassion. I have immense gratitude for what they did for me 19 years ago in the beautiful Island of Trinidad and Tobago. For not only me, but the thousands of children that came to that Centre with Spinal issues. Thank God for Dr David Toby and the Nurses! Where would we be without them.

The greatest
challenge
in life is
discovering
who you are.
The second
greatest is
being happy
with what you
find.

CHAPTER 14
MY MOTHER, MY QUEEN

Barabara my Mother was well known in her community of Lacano in Trinidad for her beauty, strength, and hard Work. Although we did not have a washing machine but a scrubbing board did the job just as well. Mother was called Washer Woman by the other women in her community because she was always washing clothes by the riverside, her clothes would always get wet in the front of her dress and it was a custom only wives of drunk husbands did this. Mom would laugh at the custom as a joke but she knew her worth as a Woman.

This was also a opportunity for the women to meet with their children to play in the river and just talk about what was happening at home.

As children came along with their moms to wash we all learnt about hard work and respect. The rocks was used to hang our clothes as they were so hug and though we did not have much, there was so much love and kindness around. We never knew we were so poor each child was told they must learn a trade so that they could do somethings as they get older so that on day they can provide for their families one day.

My mother was also a great listener and could lend an ear to anyone in need some of the women had been affected by domestic Violence and beaten up by their boyfriends and their children father. My mother was indeed very wise and always had something to say that would encourage them and build their self-esteem. Such wise words my mom would say you much get an education and learn to respect themselves.

My Mother my Queen is the loving Mother of 7 Children and 14 Gran kids and 2 Great grans in which she is very proud indeed.

Though my mother had endured great pain and hardships in her life she has been bless with also with great beauty and happiness. Her courage and support has helped her children to grow from strength to strength.

This poem describes her well

A MOTHER'S LOVE

A Mother's love is something
that no on can explain,
It is made of deep devotion
and of sacrifice and pain,
It is endless and unselfish
and enduring come what may
For nothing can destroy it
or take that love away . . .
It is patient and forgiving
when all others are forsaking,
And it never fails or falters
even though the heart is breaking . . .
It believes beyond believing
when the world around condemns,
And it glows with all the beauty
of the rarest, brightest gems . . .
It is far beyond defining,
it defies all explanation,
And it still remains a secret
like the mysteries of creation . . .
A many splendoured miracle
man cannot understand
And another wondrous evidence
of God's tender guiding hand.

~Helen Steiner Rice~

Janelle Victry Pamphile

GOD CAN MAKE BEAUTY OUT OF MESS!

"We like plans and strategies – but God's chaotic order is far bigger than our expectations. My experience of life with God is messy and painful. But I found out that there is still beauty and purpose in my life. Life is a mix of failure and success, courage and fear, faith and doubt. Since God came into my life, my whole world has been a beautiful mess. I've been re-created by a designer who loves to recycle. My life has taken a new shape. It's characterised by light and love. It's a celebration. Even if it looks a little out of control, it belongs to a loving God who has a beautiful plan. This book is an invitation. You are invited to journey into God's creative plan to make a beautiful mess of your life and your plans. Like a master artist, He is ready to take the colours of your current life and craft them into a beauty that is beyond our comprehension." By Danielle Strickland.

CHAPTER 15
HEALING OUR LIVES SO THAT WE CAN LOVE AGAIN!

HUGS ARE THE MIRACLE DRUG

Hugging therapy is definitely a powerful way of healing . Research shows that hugging (and also laughter) is extremely effective at healing sickness, disease, loneliness, depression, anxiety and stress.

Research shows a proper deep hug, where the hearts are pressing together, can benefit you in many ways:

1. The nurturing touch of a hug builds trust and a sense of safety. This helps with open and honest communication.

2. Hugs can instantly boost oxytocin levels, which heal feelings of loneliness, isolation, and anger.

3. Holding a hug for an extended time lifts one's serotonin levels, elevating mood.

4. Hugs strengthen the immune system. The gentle pressure on the sternum creates an emotional charge. This stimulates the thymus gland, which regulates and balances the body's production of white blood cells, which keep you healthy and disease free.

5. Hugging boosts self-esteem. From the time we're born our family's touch shows us that we're loved and special. The associations of self-worth and tactile sensations from our early years are still imbedded in our nervous system as adults. The cuddles we received from our Mom and Dad while growing up remain imprinted at a cellular level, and hugs remind us at a somatic level of that. Hugs, therefore, connect us to our ability to self-love.

6. Hugging relaxes muscles. Hugs release tension in the body. Hugs can take away pain; they soothe aches by increasing circulation into the soft tissues.

7. Hugs balance out the nervous system. The galvanic skin response of someone receiving and giving a hug shows a change in skin conductance. The effect in moisture and electricity in the skin suggests a more balanced state in the nervous system - parasympathetic.

8. Hugs teach us how to give and receive. There is equal value in receiving and being receptive to warmth, as to giving and sharing. Hugs educate us how love flows both ways.

9. Hugs are so much like meditation and laughter. They teach us to let go and be present in the moment. They encourage us to flow with the energy of life. Hugs get you out of your circular thinking patterns and connect you with your heart and your feelings and your breath.

10. The energy exchange between the people hugging is an investment in the relationship. It encourages empathy and understanding. And, it's synergistic, which means the whole is more than the sum of its parts: 1 plus 1 = 3 or more! This synergy is more likely to result in win-win outcomes.

There is a saying by Virginia Satir, a respected family therapist, "We need four hugs a day for survival. We need eight hugs a day for maintenance. We need twelve hugs a day for growth." Eight or more might seem quite high, but while researching and writing this article I asked my child, "How many hugs a day do you like?" She said, "I'm not going to tell you how many I like, but it's way more than eight." That really made me smile and touched my heart. And, I realized how organic and deep the need for hugs is.

"I find that love, is a miracle drug."

CHAPTER 16
LAUGHTER HEALS YOUR LIFE

1. Lowers blood pressure

People who lower their blood pressure, even those who start at normal levels, will reduce their risk of stroke and heart attack. So grab the Sunday paper, flip to the funny pages, and enjoy your laughter medicine.

2. Reduces stress hormone levels

By reducing the level of stress hormones, you're simultaneously cutting the anxiety and stress that impacts your body. Additionally, the reduction of stress hormones may result in higher immune system performance. Just think: Laughing along as a co-worker tells a funny joke can relieve some of the day's stress and help you reap the health benefits of laughter.

3. Works your abs

One of the benefits of laughter is that it can help you tone your abs. When you are laughing, the muscles in your stomach expand and contract, similar to when you intentionally exercise your abs. Meanwhile, the muscles you are not using to laugh are getting an opportunity to relax. Add laughter to your ab routine and make getting a toned tummy more enjoyable.

4. Improves cardiac health

Laughter is a great cardio workout, especially for those who are incapable of doing other physical activity due to injury or illness. It gets your heart pumping and burns a similar amount of calories per hour as walking at a slow to moderate pace. So, laugh your heart into health.

5. Boosts T-cells

T-cells are specialized immune system cells just waiting in your body for activation. When you laugh, you activate T-cells that immediately begin to help you fight off sickness. Next time you feel a cold coming on, add chuckling to your illness prevention plan.

6. Triggers the release of endorphins

Endorphins are the body's natural painkillers. By laughing, you can release endorphins, which can help ease chronic pain and make you feel good all over.

7. Produces a general sense of well-being

Laughter can increase your overall sense of well-being. Doctors have found that people who have a positive outlook on life tend to fight diseases better than people who tend to be more negative. So smile, laugh, and live longer!

Every woman has a past. Some are physically abused. Some have violent parents. Some have pubertal issues. Some have suffered sexual abuse as a child from their own family members.

Some have messed up love stories. Some have been forced into sex in the name of love. Some have been drugged. Some were date raped. Some have been photographed without their awareness.

Some have been blackmailed by their ex-boyfriend. Some were in an abusive relationship. Some have menstrual problems. Some have a broken family. Some have gone through a divorce.

Some have an obesity issue. Some have financial droughts. Some have drug or alcohol addiction.

If you see a woman, who went through any of these but had already wiped her tears, tied her hair up, masked her sorrows with a divine smile, stood tall and strong, started walking towards her future because she still has some hope left inside her and has not given up on the concept of love that still exists in this world, do not stab her with her past. Do not confront her.

Do not slap her with more abuse. Give way for her and walk beside her. Maybe hold her hands and walk for a while.

You'll know how sweet that soul is and how strong her hopes are! You'll be amazed at how she carries herself after all her energy has been sucked out.

She need not always be only the woman next door.

She could be your own friend, your own sister, your own girlfriend, your own wife, even may be your own mother. Do not judge her by her past.

Gift her the peaceful future that she deserves. Hold her hands against the world, which knows only to judge.

Give her the love that she always yearned for.

Try to accept her the way she is.

BEAUTY OF ASHES

Isaiah 61:3 says,
"to console those who mourn in Zion, to give them beauty
for ashes, the oil of joy for mourning, the garment of praise
for the spirit of heaviness that they may be called trees of
righteousness, the planting of the Lord, that He may be
glorified."

Isn't it beautiful that God says He can give you beauty for
ashes? We love that. I think we concentrate on the beauty,
but unless you give Him your ashes, you don't get the beauty.
There is a substitution plan here. There is a plan where you
give Him your ashes. Then He, in return, gives you His
beauty. We hold onto our ashes and wonder, Why doesn't my
life change? Where is His beauty? Well, where are your ashes?
You held on to them and He couldn't give you His beauty.

What are ashes? Ashes, I believe, are the wounded parts of
our lives. Everybody has wounds; everybody has ashes--and
all kinds of them. Sometimes they happen with a family
member. There can just be every kind of a thing--a mate, your
children, your job, your church. Ashes happen every place.
Everybody gets wounded.

I think the hardest wounds to turn to the Lord are the ones
you wounded yourself with when you have done stupid
things

CHAPTER 17
16 OF MY FAVOURITE
MOTIVATIONAL QUOTES

1. "Do not wait; the time will never be 'just right.' Start where you stand, and work with whatever tools you may have at your command, and better tools will be found as you go along." —George Herbert

2. "Where there is a will, there is a way. If there is a chance in a million that you can do something, anything, to keep what you want from ending, do it. Pry the door open or, if need be, wedge your foot in that door and keep it open." —Pauline Kael

3. "Do not wait; the time will never be 'just right.' Start where you stand, and work with whatever tools you may have at your command, and better tools will be found as you go along." —George Herbert

4. "Press forward. Do not stop, do not linger in your journey, but strive for the mark set before you." —George Whitefield

5. "The future belongs to those who believe in the beauty of

their dreams." —Eleanor Roosevelt

6. "Aim for the moon. If you miss, you may hit a star."
—W. Clement Stone

7. "Don't watch the clock; do what it does. Keep going."
—Sam Levenson

8 "There will be obstacles. There will be doubters. There will
be mistakes. But with hard work, there are no limits." —
Michael Phelps

9. "Keep your eyes on the stars, and your feet on the
ground." —Theodore Roosevelt

10. "We aim above the mark to hit the mark." —Ralph
Waldo Emerson

11. "One way to keep momentum going is to have constantly
greater goals." —Michael Korda

12. "Change your life today. Don't gamble on the future, act
now, without delay." —Simone de Beauvoir

13. "You just can't beat the person who never gives up." —
Babe Ruth

14. "Start where you are. Use what you have. Do what you
can." —Arthur Ashe

15. "Why should you continue going after your dreams?
Because seeing the look on the faces of the people who said
you couldn't... will be priceless." —Kevin Ngo

16. "Never give up, for that is just the place and time that the
tide will turn." —Harriet Beecher Stow

CHAPTER 18
QUOTES THAT WILL INSPIRE YOU TO BE

As entrepreneurs, leaders, and bosses, we must realize that everything we think about we are projecting into the future.

Read on to find the words of wisdom that will inspire your heart, motivate your mind in building your business, leading your life, creating success, achieving your goals, and overcoming your fears.

Quotes That Will Inspire You To Be Successful:

1. If you want to achieve greatness stop asking for permission. ~Anonymous

2. Things work out best for those who make the best of how things work out. ~John Wooden

3. To live a creative life, we must lose our fear of being wrong. ~Anonymous

4. If you are not willing to risk the usual you will have to settle for the ordinary. ~Jim Rohn

5. Trust because you are willing to accept the risk, not because it's safe or certain. ~Anonymous

6. Take up one idea. Make that one idea your life - think of it, dream of it, live on that idea. Let the brain, muscles, nerves, every part of your body, be full of that idea, and just leave every other idea alone. This is the way to success. ~Swami Vivekananda

7. All our dreams can come true if we have the courage to pursue them. ~Walt Disney

8. Good things come to people who wait, but better things come to those who go out and get them. ~Anonymous

9. If you do what you always did, you will get what you always got. ~Anonymous

10. Success is walking from failure to failure with no loss of enthusiasm. ~Winston Churchill

11. Just when the caterpillar thought the world was ending, he turned into a butterfly. ~Proverb

12. Successful entrepreneurs are givers and not takers of positive energy. ~Anonymous

13. Whenever you see a successful person you only see the public glories, never the private sacrifices to reach them. ~Vaibhav Shah

14. Opportunities don't happen, you create them. ~Chris Grosser

15. Try not to become a person of success, but rather try to become a person of value. ~Albert Einstein

16. Great minds discuss ideas; average minds discuss events; small minds discuss people. ~Eleanor Roosevelt

17. I have not failed. I've just found 10,000 ways that won't work. ~Thomas A. Edison

18. If you don't value your time, neither will others. Stop giving away your time and talents- start charging for it. ~Kim Garst

19. A successful man is one who can lay a firm foundation with the bricks others have thrown at him. ~David Brinkley

20. No one can make you feel inferior without your consent. ~Eleanor Roosevelt

21. The whole secret of a successful life is to find out what is one's destiny to do, and then do it. ~Henry Ford

22. If you're going through hell keep going. ~Winston Churchill

23. The ones who are crazy enough to think they can change the world, are the ones that do. ~Anonymous

24. Don't raise your voice, improve your argument. ~Anonymous

25. What seems to us as bitter trials are often blessings in disguise.~ Oscar Wilde

26. The meaning of life is to find your gift. The purpose of life is to give it away. ~Anonymous

27. The distance between insanity and genius is measured only by success. ~Bruce Feirstein

28. When you stop chasing the wrong things you give the right things a chance to catch you. ~Lolly Daskal

29. Don't be afraid to give up the good to go for the great. ~John D. Rockefeller

30. No masterpiece was ever created by a lazy artist.~ Anonymous

31. Happiness is a butterfly, which when pursued, is always beyond your grasp, but which, if you will sit down quietly, may alight upon you. ~Nathaniel Hawthorne

32. If you can't explain it simply, you don't understand it well enough. ~Albert Einstein

33. Blessed are those who can give without remembering and take without forgetting. ~Anonymous

34. Do one thing every day that scares you. ~Anonymous

35. What's the point of being alive if you don't at least try to do something remarkable. ~Anonymous

36. Life is not about finding yourself. Life is about creating yourself. ~Lolly Daskal

37. Nothing in the world is more common than unsuccessful people with talent. ~Anonymous

38. Knowledge is being aware of what you can do. Wisdom is knowing when not to do it. ~Anonymous

39. Your problem isn't the problem. Your reaction is the problem. ~Anonymous

40. You can do anything, but not everything. ~Anonymous

41. Innovation distinguishes between a leader and a follower. ~Steve Jobs

42. There are two types of people who will tell you that you cannot make a difference in this world: those who are afraid to try and those who are afraid you will succeed. ~Ray Goforth

43. Thinking should become your capital asset, no matter whatever ups and downs you come across in your life. ~Dr. APJ Kalam

44. I find that the harder I work, the more luck I seem to have. ~Thomas Jefferson

45. The starting point of all achievement is desire. ~Napolean Hill

46. Success is the sum of small efforts, repeated day-in and day-out. ~Robert Collier

47. If you want to achieve excellence, you can get there today. As of this second, quit doing less-than-excellent work. ~Thomas J. Watson

48. All progress takes place outside the comfort zone. ~Michael John Bobak

49. You may only succeed if you desire succeeding; you may only fail if you do not mind failing. ~Philippos

50. Courage is resistance to fear, mastery of fear - not absense of fear. ~Mark Twain

51. Only put off until tomorrow what you are willing to die having left undone. ~Pablo Picasso

52. People often say that motivation doesn't last. Well, neither does bathing - that's why we recommend it daily. ~Zig Ziglar

53. We become what we think about most of the time, and that's the strangest secret. ~Earl Nightingale

54. The only place where success comes before work is in the dictionary. ~Vidal Sassoon

55. The best reason to start an organization is to make meaning; to create a product or service to make the world a better place. ~Guy Kawasaki

56. I find that when you have a real interest in life and a curious life, that sleep is not the most important thing.~Martha Stewart

57. It's not what you look at that matters, it's what you see. ~Anonymous

58. The road to success and the road to failure are almost exactly the same. ~Colin R. Davis

59. The function of leadership is to produce more leaders, not more followers. ~Ralph Nader

60. Success is liking yourself, liking what you do, and liking how you do it. ~Maya Angelou

61. As we look ahead into the next century, leaders will be those who empower others. ~Bill Gates

62. A real entrepreneur is somebody who has no safety net underneath them. ~Henry Kravis

63. The first step toward success is taken when you refuse to be a captive of the environment in which you first find yourself. ~Mark Caine

64. People who succeed have momentum. The more they succeed, the more they want to succeed, and the more they find a way to succeed. Similarly, when someone is failing, the tendency is to get on a downward spiral that can even become a self-fulfilling prophecy. ~Tony Robbins

65. When I dare to be powerful - to use my strength in the service of my vision, then it becomes less and less important whether I am afraid. ~Audre Lorde

66. Whenever you find yourself on the side of the majority, it is time to pause and reflect. ~Mark Twain

67. The successful warrior is the average man, with laser-like focus. ~Bruce Lee

68. Take up one idea. Make that one idea your life — think of it, dream of it, live on that idea. Let the brain, muscles, nerves, every part of your body, be full of that idea, and just leave every other idea alone. This is the way to success. ~Swami Vivekananda

69. Develop success from failures. Discouragement and failure are two of the surest stepping stones to success. ~Dale Carnegie

70. If you don't design your own life plan, chances are you'll fall into someone else's plan. And guess what they have

planned for you? Not much. ~ Jim Rohn

71. If you genuinely want something, don't wait for it — teach yourself to be impatient. ~Gurbaksh Chahal

72. Don't let the fear of losing be greater than the excitement of winning. ~Robert Kiyosaki

73. If you want to make a permanent change, stop focusing on the size of your problems and start focusing on the size of you! ~T. Harv Eker

74. You can't connect the dots looking forward; you can only connect them looking backwards. So you have to trust that the dots will somehow connect in your future. You have to trust in something - your gut, destiny, life, karma, whatever. This approach has never let me down, and it has made all the difference in my life. ~Steve Jobs

75. Successful people do what unsuccessful people are not willing to do Don't wish it were easier, wish you were better. ~Jim Rohn

76. The number one reason people fail in life is because they listen to their friends, family, and neighbors. ~Napoleon Hill

77. The reason most people never reach their goals is that they don't define them, or ever seriously consider them as believable or achievable. Winners can tell you where they are going, what they plan to do along the way, and who will be sharing the adventure with them. ~Denis Watiley

78. In my experience, there is only one motivation, and that is desire. No reasons or principle contain it or stand against it. ~Jane Smiley

79. Success does not consist in never making mistakes but in never making the same one a second time. ~George Bernard Shaw

80. I don't want to get to the end of my life and find that I lived just the length of it. I want to have lived the width of it as well. ~Diane Ackerman

81. You must expect great things of yourself before you can do them. ~Michael Jordan

82. Motivation is what gets you started. Habit is what keeps you going. ~Jim Ryun

83. People rarely succeed unless they have fun in what they are doing. ~Dale Carnegie

84. There is no chance, no destiny, no fate, that can hinder or control the firm resolve of a determined soul. ~Ella Wheeler Wilcox

85. Our greatest fear should not be of failure but of succeeding at things in life that don't really matter. ~Francis Chan

86. You've got to get up every morning with determination if you're going to go to bed with satisfaction. ~George Lorimer

87. To be successful you must accept all challenges that come your way. You can't just accept the ones you like.~Mike Gafka

88. Success is...knowing your purpose in life, growing to reach your maximum potential, and sowing seeds that benefit others. ~ John C. Maxwell

89. Be miserable. Or motivate yourself. Whatever has to be done, it's always your choice. ~Wayne Dyer

90. To accomplish great things, we must not only act, but also dream, not only plan, but also believe.~ Anatole France

91. Most of the important things in the world have been accomplished by people who have kept on trying when there seemed to be no help at all. ~Dale Carnegie

92. You measure the size of the accomplishment by the obstacles you had to overcome to reach your goals. ~Booker T. Washington

93. Real difficulties can be overcome; it is only the imaginary ones that are unconquerable. ~Theodore N. Vail

94. It is better to fail in originality than to succeed in imitation. ~Herman Melville

95. Fortune sides with him who dares. ~Virgil

96. Little minds are tamed and subdued by misfortune; but great minds rise above it. ~Washington Irving

97. Failure is the condiment that gives success its flavor. ~Truman Capote

98. Don't let what you cannot do interfere with what you can do. ~John R. Wooden

99. You may have to fight a battle more than once to win it. ~Margaret Thatcher

100. A man can be as great as he wants to be. If you believe in yourself and have the courage, the determination, the

dedication, the competitive drive and if you are willing to sacrifice the little things in life and pay the price for the things that are worthwhile, it can be done. ~Vince Lombardi

positive thoughts
generate
positive feelings
and attract
positive life
experiences

CHAPTER 19
MY KNIGHT IN SHINING ARMOUR

My husband not only provides, is an outstanding father, loves me unconditionally but can stand tall alongside me in the face of tragedy. I am beyond proud to call him mine. My real life knight in shining armor

It is the Lord's doing to have kept us together in peace and love despite ups and downs here and there but Abba Father never let us down and still counting. I give thanks to God today and always for our lives. May the Lord Almighty bless us, grant us enough strength and wisdom to witness more fruitful years in good health with a sound mind and lots of celebrations. We are a happy and victorious couple, God is our rock and we have more blessings to come to us. The best is yet to come.

CHAPTER 20
CREATIVE CHICK FLORIST
JANELLE

FAMOUS FRIEND

It was a pleasure to meet Robert Winston, currently professor of Science and Society at the Imperial College London. He is a world -renowned expert in fertility and genetics. Also a BAFTA-winning broadcaster, Author and peer in the House of Lords and the Vice-President of the Royal College of Music. He is the most humble man you can ever meet.

CELEBRATING WOMEN IN MY COMMUNITY

Great experience organising this event to Inspire Women in my Community Affected by Domestic Violence and bringing people together to Celebrate... We were joined by many professionals from such a range of backgrounds, all in the name of sharing knowledge and experience as well as inspiring the future .Few people talk about - domestic abuse and honour-based violence. With 2 women dying every week in the UK due to domestic violence and an estimated 2.1 million men and women suffering domestic abuse in the UK, it really should be talked about more. I've learnt so much today, and heard some really moving personal experiences - Linus and the team you should be so proud of yourself for making it all happen

I wake up every day and remind myself. I can do this.

I have found peace in my life

Inspired by my pain.

The only thing holding you back from greatness...is you. So stop doubting yourself and do what makes you happy. Don't let anyone tell you that you can't accomplish anything! The sky's the limit my darlings!

Janelle Victry Pamphile

My Charity Kind

Kids In Need of Direction

Beauty lives in me..

I am joined with the Mayor of Redbridge and Ilford SDA Church Clerk Debbie at our Trinidad and Tobago 127 years of Adventism in London..

I love life and the beauty and creativity it brings at Carnival time in London.

Family is a great part of my life

This was a massive event I did to celebrate 125 years of Adventist History. July 22nd 2015

At our Christmas Event for Trinidad 2016

Me and my many Awards

I was Awarded this cup for my public speaking and Community projects Supporting Charites such as; Women Affected by Domestic Violence & Addiction at a Business Conference and Networking Event.

Victory is Sweet!! I am the Winner of the **Stardust** Award &2017..
Thank you to all my friend around the world that supported me.

So happy my story is shared in the Sovereign Global Magazine for Executive and Leading Entrepreneurs around the world to encourage and motivate lives

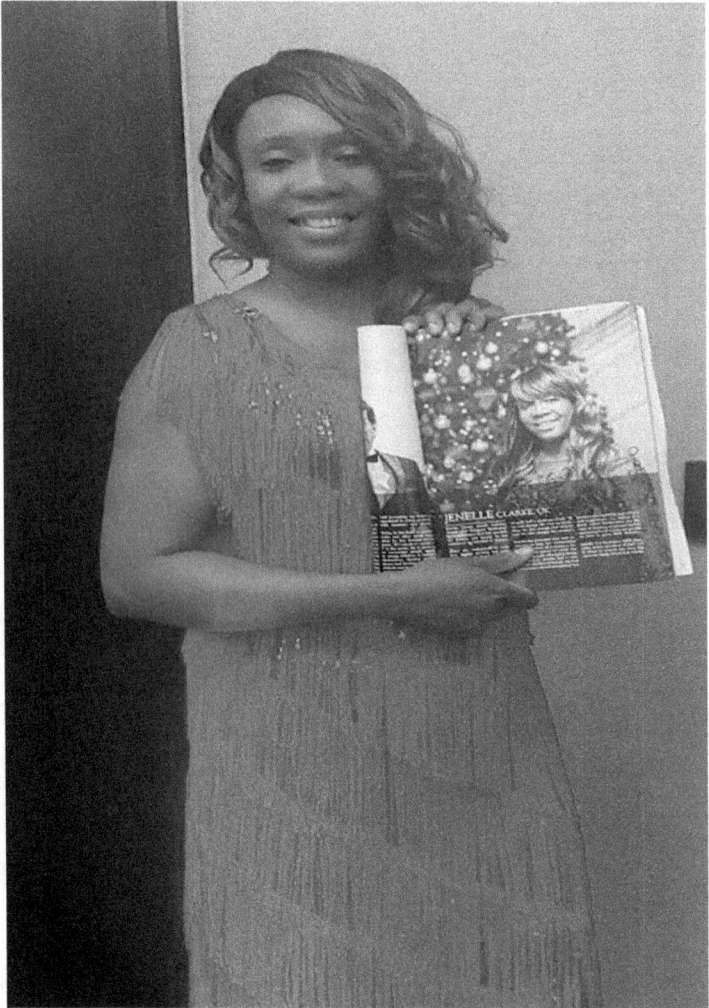

Champion and Awards Winners 2017

**Woman On a Mission: Janelle Victory Supporting
Families Affected by Domestic Violence And Addiction..
With Cllr Parvez Ahmed (Former Mayor of Brent.. I am
Blessed with a Beautiful Soul and a golden Vision.
Janelle is an Amazing Woman on a Mission to Help
Others.**

LETTER FROM HER MAJESTY THE QUEEN

**My supportive amazing Aunt Erica Daniel who is my
rock.**

**You Only Need 1 Person to Believe in You
One person to get you.
That's just the way business and life works.**

GETTING CREATIVE AT THE RITZ HOTEL IN LONDON

ABOUT THE AUTHOR

Janelle Shelly Victory Clarke Pamphile was born in the beautiful Caribbean Island of Trinidad and Tobago to a family with a large number of siblings from different ethnicities.

Her mother Barbara still lives in Trinidad. Her father; a Chronic Alcoholic had a good job at Neal and Massy as a Mechanical engineer.

When she migrated to London, it really changed her life. She has always been a visionary person since childhood.

REFERENCES

- Quotes by Lisa Nichols

- References from Lisa Nichols "What success means to me"

- Quotes from Mike Nicols

- References from Dave Carke

- References from David Toby

- References from Daniellia Stricken

- References from Elisabeth Kubler-Ross

- References from K. Payne

- Quotes from www.pinterest.com

- Poem by Hellen Steiner Rice

Janelle Victry Pamphile

www.ingramcontent.com/pod-product-compliance
Lightning Source LLC
Chambersburg PA
CBHW060514030426
42337CB00015B/1883